The Formula for Successful Marketing

Avant® Leadership Guide Series

The Formula for Successful Marketing

Complete Guide for
Marketing Professionals

Ralph Mroz

Avant Books®
San Marcos, California

Library of Congress Catalog Card Number 90-53179

ISBN 0-932238-51-3

Avant Books®
San Marcos, CA 92069-1436

Printed in the United States

Interior Design Bill McLaughlin
Art by Estay Heustis

1 2 3 4 5 6 7 8 9 10

To the late Wendell R. Smith (former partner in Booz, Allen, Hamilton, former Vice President of RCA, and former Dean of the University of Massachusetts Business School), the professor who made me realize that maybe there is something to this marketing stuff after all.

Table of Contents

Preface

The purpose of this book is to describe all of the interlocking elements of marketing while placing them into a structure that reveals the relationships between those elements. This effort grew out of my consulting experience. I found that I was leaving my clients lists of marketing activities, and it occurred to me that the lists were all pretty similar. I decided it was time to write a definitive list of all marketing activities, as my own marketing crib sheet. Structured in a useful way, this list became a marketing formula. That model is presented in the first part of this book.

This is not a marketing how-to book. There are many excellent books and references on that extensive subject, and I don't have anything original to contribute to it. You will not, for example, learn how to do market research in this book. You will, however, find all of the elements of market research.

It is my hope that marketing professionals will be able to do their jobs a little more easily and a little more completely, and that general management will be helped in setting expectations from marketing.

Acknowledgments

Thanks to my former bosses, who were patient while I learned all of this. Particular thanks are due Barbara Chapin who contributed valuable ideas.

About the Author

Ralph Mroz is the principal consultant at Iris Development, Sterling, Massachusetts, a management consulting firm specializing in marketing and strategic planning. He has done or managed just about every marketing function there is. His responsibilities at one company allowed him to observe marketing from the customer's point of view.

Working in many different marketing and strategic planning positions, Mr. Mroz has been employed by such giants as Hewlett-Packard Company and Digital Equipment Corporation. He has also had the experience of involvement with start-up operations including Encore Computer Corporation.

Mroz has a BS in Electrical Engineering and an MBA with an Industrial Marketing concentration.

Part One

The Model

Chapter 1

Understanding Marketing

This book provides a model for the entire marketing function, and lists all of its activities. If you are a marketing professional, it will furnish a formula for your activities; if you work in another area or are a general manager, it will provide a set of guidelines for working with and evaluating marketing.

The Need

Marketing is the function that provides the link between the business and the rest of the world. It is the translator between the needs, trends, and practices of the outside world and the capabilities of the business. It is, by definition, impossible for any business to function without such a link.

Whether you are concerned about the success of a huge or tiny company, marketing is one of the functions that, like bookkeeping, must be done in order for the company to achieve that success.

If you want to make a profit, whether you are a marketing professional, a member of general management, part of a small (or even one-person) shop, or an entrepreneur starting a business, marketing must be of vital concern to you. You must understand it, it's elements, the arrangement of those elements, and the relationships between them. In short, you must have a model of marketing to allow you to develop a blueprint for your own particular marketing needs.

The Problem

Even though the need is great, marketing professionals and business managers seldom understand the full spectrum of marketing activities, both strategic and tactical. They don't understand the relationship of these activities with respect to each other and with respect to the other functions within their firm and the external environment.

The Consequences

The situations are all too familiar:

An established company, no longer a young *start up*, is beginning to falter. Growth isn't what it was, profit margins are falling and customers are not as wild about the products as they once were. The original management is finally trying some new marketing approaches—a new approach every quarter it seems—and none are very successful.

The new technology start-up company, staffed with experienced people from established companies, has a hot new product. The management has a healthy respect for marketing, but has some trouble describing just what it is, and the marketing effort seems a little sluggish getting off the ground. In any case, the focus of effort always seems to be on product and technology issues.

Your company is introducing a new product, or a new product line is being formed, or a new market is being targeted for the company's products. A marketing plan is needed and a lot of management time is used determining what *marketing* will be, *this time*.

The mature firm—comfortably profitable for so long—is seeing its margins erode in the face of rapid market change, and customers are being lost to more nimble competitors. The firm understands that it has been a bit lax in its past marketing efforts and wants to rectify the situation. But where to begin? What is marketing, anyway?

Do these scenarios sound familiar? If so, you're not alone. Most companies have a great deal of difficulty in articulating, organizing and executing marketing. Indeed, most would be hard pressed to define marketing in a meaningful way.

Yet environmental, technological, competitive, and regulatory forces are compelling firms to change more quickly and respond faster, with greater effectiveness than ever before. These forces have correctly propelled marketing to the forefront of most company's concerns.

The Need for a Model

Most human activities are so complex that we require some sort of model or blueprint in order to manage or perform them effectively. A model is a tool that defines an activity, delineates its components in an orderly manner, and defines the relationships between the components.

No one would think of constructing a house or building without a complete set of blueprints, yet we routinely build marketing staffs and engage in marketing activities without knowing exactly what marketing is, what all of its elements are, and how the elements are related.

Many familiar problems are caused by this lack of a universal model for marketing:

No one understands what marketing is. One of the most frequently heard questions in the corporate environment is "What *is* marketing, anyway?" No such confusion exists in other well-defined activities. No one asks "What is manufacturing?" or "What is sales?" To be sure, there is often great confusion about the most effective way to perform these functions, but there is little confusion about their basic nature, their primary activity, and their relationship to the rest of the firm.

It is very difficult to perform any activity effectively—much less manage it—without an overall model of the task. The old saying about "knowing where you're going before you start out" got to be an old saying because of its basic truth.

In a corporate setting "knowing where you're going" means knowing the necessary activities to perform, understanding their context, and understanding the relationships between those activities. Models are the tools that provide that information.

Marketing is constantly being re-invented. A painfully familiar phenomenon is that a great deal of the firm's time is used determining what the marketing should consist of for each new product or market. This constant re-invention is necessitated by the absence of a universal, comprehensive model of marketing. Because there is no such model, a change in one variable (such as the product, or target market) usually invalidates the entire existing marketing structure and a new one must be created. The purpose of models is to prevent this kind of fruitless re-invention.

Resources are mis-appropriated. Marketing is a part of the overall corporate effort and it will not be properly funded if its place is not fully understood. Resource allocation, in a corporate context, means primarily money and people. When an engineering manager wants more money or people, he or she has no problem identifying the project and no one has a problem understanding the trade-offs involved in allocation or non-allocation of the resources. This understanding is possible because the role of engineering activities are well understood.

The marketing manager, on the other hand, usually has a difficult time articulating the need for marketing expenditures. This is because there is not a general understanding of the role and context of marketing - in other words, there is not a good model of the overall marketing function.

Marketing activities are performed inefficiently. If we view the corporation as a system with inputs and outputs, then its larger activities, such as marketing, can be viewed as major subsystems. Major subsystems are composed of minor subsystems—such as the different classes or types of activities. If a major subsystem (marketing) is not working properly with other major subsystems (engineering, sales, etc.), the overall system (the corporation) does not perform optimally. Likewise, if the minor subsystems (classes of marketing activities) within a major subsystem (marketing) are not in proper alignment with each other, the major subsystem (marketing) malfunctions, causing the entire system (the corporation) to falter.

This sort of inefficiency is commonly observed in the form of scattered and unconnected marketing programs, overlaps of marketing activities and gaps between them, and poor coordination with other departments such as product development and sales.

Corporate underperformance is avoided by utilizing a comprehensive, integrated model that relates major subsystems to each other and structures the functions of minor subsystems within a major subsystem. The major corporate subsystem of marketing usually underperforms because of the lack of a comprehensive model defining these relationships.

The failure of a product or business. Today, marketing is often acknowledged as the most important function in a firm. Therefore, the failure of marketing generally means the failure of the product or firm. The firms succumbing recently, and sometimes spectacularly, to such a fate is well-documented.

Inter-departmental communication and cooperation is poor. In the business world, conflicts between marketing and engineering, or between marketing and sales, are well known facts of life. It is a rare company that does not have at least some friction along these lines, and often along other marketing interfaces as well.

This conflict is not inherent in a business nor in the make-up of the individuals. Rather, it is confusion about the roles of, boundaries separating, and communication between the different departments that are the cause. Without a comprehensive model of marketing to define its activities, inter-departmental conflict is inevitable.

There is a lack of measurement criteria for marketing performance and marketing management evaluation. Without a thorough understanding of marketing and what it is supposed to do, measurement of the activities and people in marketing must be either subjective or based on false expectations. For example, how often have we seen marketing personnel rewarded (or reprimanded) solely on the basis of present sales levels, rather than long-term marketing results?

A New Approach

Many authorities have developed excellent models for some parts of the marketing function. There are excellent models available for advertising, public relations, product management, market research, and so on. There are even models for strategic marketing, the planning aspect of marketing activities. Phillip Kotler, in his widely used *Marketing Management:*

Analysis, Planning and Control, defines an excellent model of strategic marketing, a modified version of which is used in this book.

But to date, there has been no overall model of the entire marketing function encompassing the whole range of marketing operations and planning activities, relating them to each other, and placing those activities in the context of the corporate and external environment. That is what we will do in this book.

The next chapter provides a comprehensive model of marketing which:

> Defines marketing.
>
> Establishes the context of marketing vis-a-vis other corporate functions.
>
> Establishes the relationship between marketing and the external (outside the corporation) environment.
>
> Defines *marketing operations* and *marketing planning*.
>
> Defines the relationship between marketing operations and marketing planning activities.
>
> Lays the foundation for a hierarchial structuring of all marketing activities - a marketing formula.

Part Two of this book develops in detail a model for marketing operations, listing each of the 168 individual activities that make up the marketing operations formula.

Part Three develops a model of marketing planning in detail, and lists the fifty activities that make up the marketing planning formula.

Part Four details the entire Marketing Formula.

Part Five explains how to put these models and formulas to work and explores the implications of this new understanding for management, marketing professionals, and the organization.

Is Marketing Really Worthwhile?

Since marketing is the link between the enterprise and the rest of the world, it is impossible for any enterprise to function without it. Therefore, marketing is not just worthwhile, it is absolutely necessary. While some firms get by without the marketing function being formally established, the marketing activities are done of necessity.

In the last fifteen years several fundamental business functions have acquired and lost fad status, including strategic planning, marketing, and, most recently, manufacturing efficiency. It is, of course, imperative that these, and all, functional areas be implemented effectively for a firm to prosper, just as all of your internal organs must function effectively for you to prosper. Further, these functional activities must be practiced correctly, not merely run through the corporation as the latest fad.

Marketing has been as abused as any other activity incorrectly practiced as a fad. Recently, however, it has been undergoing a rediscovery. Many companies are learning that true marketing is essential in today's increasingly competitive climate, and they are making the investment and commitment necessary to sustain a real marketing program.

In order for any function to be effective it must have the full support of management, not just lip service. It must be practiced in context, not blindly implemented regardless of the relationship to other activities.

For example, one reason for the failure of so many companies that declared themselves *marketing driven* is that they mistook sales for marketing. This was the easy way out, requiring neither intelligent analysis nor major commitment.

Sales and marketing are two separate, although related, activities. Sales is concerned with the needs of the firm, marketing with the needs of the customer. While sales has a long-term horizon of one year, marketing has a horizon of five to ten years.

Sales is primarily an operational activity, marketing is primarily a strategic (planning) activity. Beefing up sales is a tactical activity; making a corporation *marketing driven* often requires a remaking of the firm's strategy, culture, and management style, and sometimes a remaking of the management personnel. It is often much easier for the fainthearted and shortsighted managers of some companies to simply hire a few more salespeople and make pronouncements about being *customer driven* than it is to correct the serious organizational deficiencies that plague their firms.

A Marketing Formula?

Marketing. The word conjures up images of a job of vast creativity and people with a magical intuitive understanding of the right thing to produce or the right way to promote it.

Bunk.

Marketing is like any other professional activity. Ninety percent of it consists of predicable activities; that is, ninety percent of it can be put into a formula. The remaining ten percent, of course, does require a broad and intuitive understanding of the business and creative insight into it. But that ten percent can't be done properly if the foundation hasn't been laid with the other ninety percent of time and effort.

In this respect, marketing is similar to most professional areas of work. Doctors must spend a good deal of their time obtaining accurate routine test results that is combined with their knowledge and experience in order to make an accurate diagnosis and prescription for treatment. An accountant must have accurate and complete financial and cost accounting data in order to make the proper choices in allocating funds and expenses. The marketing person must also have a great deal of information at hand in order to make wise decisions regarding major strategies.

When the routine part of the job is done completely and effectively, the creative aspect of the job becomes much easier. All the data from which important conclusions can be drawn are laid out clearly. All of the relevant facts are available, and patterns are apparent.

Chapter 2

A Comprehensive Model of Marketing

This chapter will develop an overall model for the marketing function. This comprehensive model will serve as a guide to the complex web of individual activities that compose marketing. In later chapters we will fully discuss these specific, individual activities.

Rather than jump right into the individual activities it is important to understand this comprehensive model first. We can see why by considering a pilot. He must study the principles of flying and understand the relationships between the forces that affect the airplane before he flys. This understanding allows him to perform the individual flying activities in an orderly manner, as part of a larger set of coordinated activities. Gaining this initial understanding is far preferable to jumping into the plane and doing individual activities at random!

The model starts with the definition of marketing at the beginning of this book:

Marketing is the function that provides the link between the business and the rest of the world. It is the translator between the needs, trends, and practices of the outside world and the capabilities of the business.

Starting from that definition, the comprehensive model is a union of two models: a model of marketing operations and a model of marketing planning. We first outline a model of marketing operations (which we will develop fully in Part Two of this book).

Onto the operations model we build a model of marketing planning (developed fully in Part Three), producing a model for the overall marketing function. This overall model must then be placed into marketing's environment: the rest of the firm and the external environment. We do this by defining the flows of information between the two components of the model and their environments.

Marketing Operations vs. Marketing Planning

Marketing planning is an activity which defines the overall marketing direction. It generally consists of those marketing activities that are concerned with the fundamental and/or long term marketing issues. Typical planning questions are: "What should our product set be in five years?", "How are the opportunities in the market changing?", and "How should we enter a new market?"

The term *strategic marketing* is often bantered around, often without a clear understanding of its meaning. By Webster's definition, strategic is an adjective that refers to an overall plan or set of planning activities. *Strategic marketing* is therefore marketing planning, they mean the same thing.

Marketing operations (or *tactical marketing*) is concerned with the performance of marketing activities, i.e., the implementation of marketing plans. It is the nuts and bolts of marketing. Activities like current advertising campaigns, market research, and product introductions are often marketing operations activities.

It is tempting to conclude that the operations vs. planning distinction is one of long term vs. short term time spans. Indeed, the distinction between them is often erroneously defined that way. That distinction is sometimes true but it is not generally valid; at times planning priorities group neatly into long term horizons and operational activities into shorter term horizons, but this is not always the case.

For instance, day to day advertising is usually considered an operational concern, but consider a company whose future hinges on gaining market share this year. That short term effort is very important within the marketing planning function. Or consider a long term issue, such as the specific location of future distribution sites. This is often a serious planning concern to retailing operations, but not something of great planning importance to, say, many manufacturing firms.

In fact, the differentiation between operations and planning is one of setting direction vs. following the direction; navigation vs. piloting.

A Marketing Operations Model

Models delineate and organize elements of a system (in this case, marketing operations). At the topmost level, marketing operations activities are divided into four major areas:

- **Understand** the environment.
- **Predict** the environment.
- **Develop** products within the firm to mesh with the needs and desires of the entities composing the environment.
- **Promote** the developed products to the environment.

Each of these four major areas is itself composed of four sub-areas as follows:

- Understand the
  - market
  - customer
  - competition
  - products
- Predict the
  - market
  - customer
  - competition
  - products

- Develop within the firm
  - products
  - expectations
  - investments
  - organizational structure
- Promote
  - products
  - the firm
  - sales to prospects
  - customer partnerships

Each of these sixteen sub-areas can be broken down further into the activities that compose them, for a total of 168 marketing activities that make up marketing operations. For example:

Understand competitors is broken down into twenty-one activities such as: defining the characteristics of the competitors, understanding why competitors customers are their customers, understanding competitors' terms and conditions, understanding their manufacturing strengths, and so on.

Promote products is divided into ten activities such as: media advertising, product documentation, and so on.

These marketing operations tasks are usually performed by groups such as market research, advertising, product management, and so on.

A Marketing Planning Model

How do we make the leap from *Understand and Predict* to *Develop and Promote*? How do we use the understandings and predictions to turn them into products and promotions?

Making that connection requires planning, and marketing planning is the activity that does it. A general planning model serves quite well to define marketing planning:

- Identify Opportunities
- Set Objectives
- Develop Strategy
- Formulate Plans
- Implement and Control

For marketing, we can break these five major areas down further and further until we finally reveal all of the fifty individual marketing planning activities. But for now, it is enough to understand that marketing planning consists of those five broad areas.

These activities are often performed by groups with names such as market development, strategic planning, and—of course—market planning.

A Comprehensive Model

Combining the models of marketing planning and marketing operations produces a model for the overall marketing function.

Adding to that overall model, the context of the rest of the firm and the external environment, as well as the relationships between the elements of the model, produces the comprehensive model of marketing in Figure 2-1. The arrows in the figure represent information flows which define the relationships between the model's elements.

The flow of information between the components of the model constitute an input-output relationship between the parts. For example, *Understand and Predict* is an activity characterized by a flow of information from the environment and the rest of the firm to the Understand and Predict functions within marketing. These two marketing functions (Understand *and* Predict) reduce and analyze this data and output the analysis to the *Identify Opportunities*, *Set Objectives*, and *Develop Strategy* functions within the marketing planning area. These areas in turn transform this analysis into information that will influence other activities.

The Set Objectives function uses that input and the input from *Identify Opportunities* to set marketing objectives, and outputs those objectives to the *Develop Strategy* area, which combines those objectives with the input from the *Understand and Predict* functions to output the strategies used

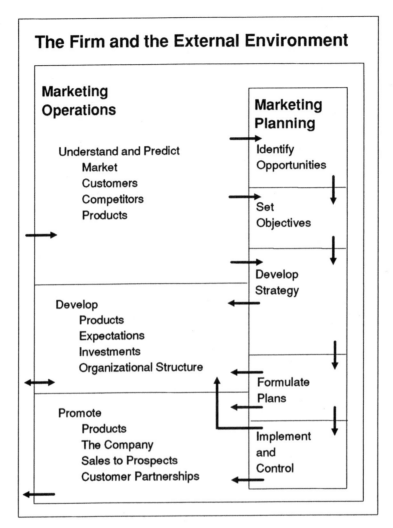

Figure 2-1   A Comprehensive Model of Marketing

as starting points for the *Formulate Plans* activity. The *Develop Strategy* and *Formulate Plans* functions both output information to the *Develop* function in the form of directions for products, investments, expectations and organizational structure. The *Develop* function, in turn, must output information to the rest of the firm (e.g. the product development department) and the external environment in order to accomplish these tasks.

The *Formulate Plans* function directs information in the form of plans to the *Implement and Control* so that it can devise means of performing and monitoring these plans. Both of these functions output information to the *Develop* and *Promote* areas, setting direction for the development of products, expectations, investments, and organizational structure, and the promotion of products, the company, sales to prospects and customer partnerships. The operational *Promote* and *Develop* activities finally direct information outward to the external environment. *Promote* directs information outward primarily to potential customers and also to the rest of the firm (sales training, for example). *Develop* directs information outward to the product development function within the firm and to contractors and suppliers that the firm must work with.

A New Understanding

Now we have an overall idea of what's involved in marketing. We can see the major components of marketing planning and of marketing operations, and see how they relate. It is now apparent that marketing is not a set of undefined, intuitive activities. Like any other function, it is composed of specific activities and these activities work together in a particular way

We now need to examine in detail the activities that make up each of the major components of marketing. Part Two of this book will describe marketing operations. Part Three will cover marketing planning. Part Five will examine how to put these formulas to work in your organization.

Part Two

The Marketing Operations
Formula

Chapter 3

The Understand Formula

What you need to understand is the total environment in which you are conducting business, and that's often a lot broader than you may think. An organization exists in some context, and its activities consist of effectively managing relationships within that context. To do this, the organization must have eyes and ears on the rest of the world, and this is one of marketing's jobs.

In Figure 2-1, there are four items listed below *Understand*: Market, Customers, Competitors, and Products. Understanding these items is primarily a matter of gathering information. Of course, considerable creativity is often required in obtaining and interpreting this information.

Understanding the Market—Twenty Four Items

The first thing to understand is the market for your products in terms of the classical segmentations. This will give you a broadbrush view of the state of the industry.

Remember, though, that markets are hierarchial. You will also find it helpful to understand the larger markets of which your market is a subset (these are called super-markets). For example, if you manufacture office desks, you will not only care about the characteristics of the desk market (the market), you will also be concerned about the characteristics of the larger office supplies market (the super-market), of which the office desk market is a subset.

Markets are usually looked at and segmented in three ways: by dollar sales, by units sold, and by dollar profits. All the following segmentations should be done along all three lines.

First you have to know the overall market size (in dollar sales, unit sales, and profits) as well as the dollar sales and unit sales of the super-market. You will then need to segment the market (again, in terms of sales volume, in terms of units, and in terms of profits) by competitor, customer type, geography, and sales channel. Your industry knowledge and experience will have to be used to determine how you segment, for example, customer type; that is an example of the creative aspect of your job.

Next, you need to apply your knowledge to determine other specific segmentations that make sense for your industry - perhaps you need to segment by price bands, or product functions, or manufacturing process used, whatever makes sense for your particular industry. Again, the whole picture requires that this segmentation be done by sales volume, by units, and by profit.

The easiest way to look at this information is in the form of pie charts, using one pie chart for each segmentation. That's a lot of data, a lot of pie charts to generate. But, by representing the market data all these ways you use the tremendous ability of the generated charts to reveal the fundamental relationships of those markets. You can clearly see the distribution of sales and profits, which competitors and products are strong and in what areas, where the opportunities lie, and so on. This is the kind of information that is necessary to decide what products to develop and what promotional strategies are needed.

You're not done. You will also need to know the dynamics of all that information you've gathered and put into pie charts; that is, you need to know the rate at which each of the numbers is changing. This doubles the amount of data you will generate, but much more than doubles the amount of information conveyed. This exercise tells you not just how the world is, but how and in what direction it is changing.

In addition to knowing how the market is structured and changing, you will need to know something about the rest of the businesses that have an influence on the market. These important influences are usually the technology involved in the products and how it's changing, and the manufacturing process and materials used and how they are changing. Perhaps there are other influences in your industry. Your own experience and knowledge must be used to determine which are important. These influences need to be understood and segmented, perhaps along the lines discussed above, perhaps along others.

You will have already cut the market's profit various ways, so you understand what the returns are in your industry and how they are changing from several different angles, but you may also want to investigate how the financial structure of the market and the players are changing. For instance, is the industry becoming more capital intensive? Are sales expenses increasing? What are the profit margins and how are they changing? What are returns and where are they going? And so on down the financial checklist. Again, your experience and knowledge will tell you which financial aspects of the industry you need to spend time researching and which are not so important. This information can help to anticipate necessary changes in your operation, predict future moves of competitors, and understand changes in the source of profitability.

Understanding the market is done by gathering information. This information comes from several sources: your own knowledge, associates, market research departments, market research companies, salespeople, financial analysts, periodicals, government studies, financial references (e.g., Dun and Bradstreet, Standard and Poors), as well as others. Part of the job is to build a system to gather all of this information.

Understanding the Customer—Nine Things

Understanding the customer tells you what you must produce to be successful and how to offer it. You need to understand your customers and desired customers in great depth. It is, after all, their buying decisions that constitute profits. You need to offer them a package that constitutes the total product they want to buy: product, service, terms and conditions, and whatever else they deem important.

First, you need to know who your customers and potential customers are. This means you must define them. Both groups of them - there may be a difference between current customers and those you wish to be customers, as well as the people who are logical customers for your products.

You need to know why they are buying your product, why they need this kind of product, what they use it for, and if substitute products are available, thus defining their product-type-buying criteria.

You need to understand why they buy from a particular vendor, which means defining their vendor selection criteria. Is it the vendor's size, reputation, terms and conditions, delivery time, or something else that causes them to buy from one vendor and not another?

Buying patterns vary from industry to industry, and you must understand the patterns in your industry. Do customers place large or small orders? Are the orders cyclic? Are customer's product needs correlated with some variable? How else can their buying patterns be defined and classified?

Identify the decision makers in desired customer's organizations. Are they the purchasing agent, engineer, manager, company executive, or others? Understand their decision process. Is the buying decision up to one person, a group, a chain of people or groups, or is some other mechanism used?

You will need to understand in detail how the product is used in the customer's business or consumption pattern. What purpose does the product serve in their organization?

In addition, you should understand why you have won sales and why you have lost sales.

As with the market information, you also need to know how these items are changing, so you must go back and understand the dynamics of all these categories.

The gathered information is usually presented in the form of short answers to the above questions, although sometimes the answers lend themselves to graphical presentation. Graphs should always be used when possible because of the vast amount of information they convey and their unique ability to make patterns apparent. In fact, presenting in graphical form a subject that seems unsuited to it can expose patterns you might not otherwise have seen.

The information discussed here comes from many sources: industry literature, periodicals, the sales force, directly from customers, industry experts, and even commercial market research firms. Explore them all and use your creativity to build an effective system to gather information.

Oftentimes, in researching information, your knowledge of the business problems and the business itself may exceed that of the owner. This puts you in the enviable position of being able to anticipate needs and solutions to problems that the owner does not yet know exist.

Understanding the Competition—Twenty One Areas

Your competitors are out there with you, after the same customers, with many of the same resources you possess. Your job is to understand them and:

1)   Know how to capitalize on their weaknesses,

2)   Plot strategy so your product or service will be superior to theirs in some significant way.

You need to understand the following parameters and, as always, their dynamics - how they are changing:

- From your customer's point of view, who are your competitors? What are their defining characteristics? You may be surprised to learn that your real competitors are not who you thought them to be. Your competition may come from an entirely different direction, or from another product altogether.

- Through what channels do they sell? Are they the same as yours, or different? Why?

- How do they sell their product; that is, what are the sales procedures that they employ? Perhaps they always call on a particular level in the organization, use certain incentives, rely on demonstrations or employ some other kind of procedures.

- What are their terms and conditions? Are they flexible? If so, are they always flexible?
- What services do they offer with their products? Are the services free? For what period do they extend?
- What is their entire product line, and which products within it are they actively selling? What products are under development?
- Are there holes in their product line?
- What are their product strategies—which products are being phased out, being discounted, being replaced, are temporary, are loss leaders, and so on?
- What are the profit margins for the various products they sell? On which do they lose money and how much can they cut prices?
- Who are their customers and why? How stable are these customers?
- What are their promotional tactics and plans? What will be the effect of their promotion on customers?
- What are their strengths in marketing, sales, financial position, manufacturing, and technology? What are their weaknesses in those areas?

Again, this information is best displayed graphically whenever possible. And don't forget, you need this information for the present and you need to know how these situations are changing.

This information comes from lots of legwork and a good marketing information system. The legwork consists of reading and clipping articles from the industry and business press, calling the competition on the phone (you will be surprised how much they will tell you), going to trade shows, talking with former employees, listening to trade gossip, industry specialists and stock analysts, reading their literature and financial reports, using research houses, attending technical conferences and reading technical papers that they publish - as well as their employment advertisements in the newspapers and industry research reports.

The remainder of the information comes from anyone who has contact with customers or the competition or comes through a well-oiled marketing information system (Japanese firms excel at this. Until recently it was common at many Japanese firms for anyone who had contact with foreign companies to undergo an extensive debriefing. The smallest details were considered important and analyzed). Sales and service people are usually the ones to pick up information from customers and users of your product. Technical people also pick up useful information and, of course, marketing people are paid to do this job.

Understanding the Products—Eight Aspects

You sell a product, your customer buys a product, your competition competes with a product. You must understand the products in the marketplace so that your product will fill the market demand.

The first task is to list all the competing products in your market. Then you must organize them into as many categories and along as many dimensions as makes sense for your market. Perhaps by functions performed, perhaps by price, or by size, color, or speed. Whatever. And maybe along several of these dimensions at once (function X vs. function Y), for example, price vs. speed is a common two-dimensional product description in the computer industry. And make sure you include how all of the variables are changing.

The next step is to understand why the products are used. Why them and not something else? What are the substitute products and what prevents them from being used? How is all of this changing?

In what stage of the product-life cycle are your products? What does this tell you about costs, prices, substitute products, demand, market size, and customer characteristics? Must you ride the classic product-life cycle curve, or can you reposition your products along it?

What is the relationship of your products to other products now being used by your customers? Is one a subassembly in another, or is yours interchangeable with another? Does some other relationship exist?

What percentage of the customer's product cost or budget does your product represent? Is the functional or economic necessity of your product dependent on another product? What is changing in these other products and these relationships that affects you?

How does your product work? What makes it do what it does? Does the way it works have relevance to the customer? Is the way it works likely to change? What will your customer think of that?

The answers to these questions come, once again, from research, your development groups, and your marketing information system.

The Understand Formula

All of the following items must be understood at present in addition to the way they are changing

Understand the Market	Understand the Competitors
Size by sales	Defining characteristics
Size by units	Channels
Size by profits	Sales procedures
Super-market size by sales	Terms and conditions
Super-market size by units	Services
Competitors by sales	Product set
Competitors by units	Product strategies
Competitors by profits	Profit Margins
Customer type by sales	Customers-who
Customer type by units	Customers-why
Customer type by profits	Promotional tactics
Geography by sales	Marketing strengths
Geography by units	Sales strengths
Geography by profits	Financial strengths
Channels by sales	Manufacturing strengths
Channels by units	Technical strengths
Channels by profits	Marketing weaknesses
Specific segmentations by sales	Sales weaknesses

Understand the Market	Understand the Competitors
Specific segmentations by units	Financial weaknesses
Specific segmentations by profits	Manufacturing weaknesses
Technological influences	Technical weaknesses
Manufacturing influences	
Other influences	
Financial influences	

Understand the Customer	Understand the Products
Define existing customers	Competing products
Define potential customers	Product categories
Product type buying criteria	Why used
Vendor criteria	Substitutes
Buying patterns	Life cycle stage
Decision makers	Relation to other products
Decision process	Percentage of cost
Product use	How the product works
Sales and lost sales analysis	

Chapter 4

The Predict Formula

The last chapter focused on gathering information about the environment. That information will give you the state of the environmental characteristics affecting you, their direction and rate of change. But, because you must make and implement plans to get to a place at some later time, you need to understand how the world will look in the future. You need to know not just where you are and how things are currently changing—the things you *understood* in the last chapter—but where things will be.

Now, you must add a prediction as to where each piece of gathered information will be in the future.

The time span to predict should be the length of time that is appropriate in your industry to do strategic planning. Five years is a proper span of time for most industries but not for all businesses. The oil industry, for instance, must be concerned with the state of affairs twenty years into the future. The fashion industry, by contrast, primarily worries about time spans of only one year.

After you determine the right span of time for your business, go back to *The Understand Formula* and fill it all in again for the future.

But, don't try to cheat by simply extrapolating the rate of change for each variable that you have determined. The rate of change may itself be changing, or there may be sudden abrupt changes in some trends. In fact, that is probably the case. Very few industries plod along at the same rate year after year. There's a lot more research to do here. Some of this future information may be easy to predict, some may be known by research organizations, some by people in your organization. But it is also necessary for you to draw on your knowledge and experience in order to predict that far into the future. You want to involve many people in this process, this is a good opportunity for brainstorming sessions.

The Predict Formula

Predict The Market	Predict The Competitors
Size by sales	Defining characteristics
Size by units	Channels
Size by profits	Sales procedures
Super-market size by sales	Terms and conditions
Super-market size by units	Services
Competitors by sales	Product set
Competitors by units	Product strategies
Competitors by profits	Profit margins
Customer type by sales	Customers-who
Customer type by units	Customers-why
Customer type by profits	Promotional tactics
Geography by sales	Marketing strengths
Geography by units	Sales strengths
Geography by profits	Financial strengths
Channels by sales	Manufacturing strengths
Channels by units	Technical strengths
Channels by profits	Marketing weaknesses
Specific segmentations by sales	Sales weaknesses
Specific segmentations by units	Financial weaknesses
Specific segmentations by profits	Manufacturing weaknesses
Technological influences	Technical weaknesses
Manufacturing influences	
Other influences	
Financial influences	

Predict the Customer	Predict the Products
Future customers	Competing products
Potential customers	product categories
Product buying criteria	why used
Vendor criteria	Substitutes
Buying patterns	Life cycle stage
Decision makers	Relation to other products
Decision process	Percentage of cost
Product use	How the product works
Sales and lost sales analysis	

Chapter 5

The Develop Formula

You now understand the environment in which your company conducts business, and the relationships that exist within that environment. You also have a good idea where your world will be in the future. Now you can start to manage your organization's relationships to capitalize on the environmental situation. Now you move from analysis to action.

There are four things that need to be developed: products, expectations, investments, and organizational structure. Notice that these developmental activities take place mostly inside the organization. It is a common erroneous belief that marketing is concerned only with activities external to the firm, with the *outside world*. In fact, the job of marketing is matching the opportunities in the environment with the capabilities of the firm. Marketing is the link between the *outside world* and the *inside world*.

Marketing is directly involved in developing products because we are now in the third stage of industrial production, the marketing stage. The first stage, production, occurred during the later nineteenth century and the first decade of the twentieth century. Things—mostly basic goods—were produced because they could be produced. There was no need to worry about small details when the entire world was hungry for necessities and anxious for the rapid rise in living standards that accompanies the beginning of a modern industrial society. The scent of the soap was hardly a major buying decision when the simple availability of soap was a Godsend.

Equally on the industrial side, the detailed characteristics of steel were not as important as its easy availability. Production was the dominant orientation and function of an enterprise.

The second stage, the sales stage, roughly spans the period between the two World Wars. Basic goods were commonplace and customers—both retail and industrial—could choose from a greater variety of products. Production was coming into line with demand. After a product was made it had to be sold. Within an enterprise, sales became the dominant orientation and function.

The third stage is now, and it is marketing. Producing a good product is no longer enough, nor will any amount of sales expertise necessarily sell it. You must now go to market with exactly the product that customers want. Standards of living have risen to a point where most people in the industrialized countries have more than enough, a notion completely unthinkable a mere hundred years ago. Needs no longer drive end-use purchases, desires do.

The activities required to anticipate and match customers' desires with the capabilities of the business define the marketing function. Since the market will buy only that which it desires, it is the firm that must adapt in order for there to be a match. Therefore these adaptations—these developmental activities—are marketing's responsibility.

Developing Products—Seven Aspects

The easiest path to profitable sales is the production of products that customers want to buy. To do this, the technical developing organization—the people who design new products—must work hand-in-hand with the people who know the customer's desires: the marketing organization.

The technical organization develops the products that the marketing organization specifies. Marketing determines *what* and *when*, the technical organizations determine *how* and define the trade-offs. These areas feed back to each other in an interactive, ongoing process. Product development becomes a team effort between the marketing and technical groups. It is the responsibility of general management to ensure that the business accommodates and encourages that kind of cooperation.

This relationship applies equally to companies in the so-called *supply driven* markets. In these markets—usually high-technology—new products appear to create their own demand. Prior to their existence customers could not have conceived of them. The argument goes that it is fruitless to attempt to divine the market's desires when the individuals composing it can't imagine the products that would meet their desires. But, while customers may not be aware of a product that would meet their desires, they certainly understand what their desires are. Again, it is the job of marketing to translate those desires, whether described in terms of a product or simply a problem, into products.

The first part of developing products is to define product requirements in conjunction with the design departments. The physical product itself, however, is not the entire product that a customer buys. Service, terms and conditions, and support are other parts of the total product, and the requirements for these must be defined in conjunction with the proper departments: Service, Sales, Finance, and Product Support.

Of course products must be timely, and the proper time frames for development of these products must be defined by marketing and communicated to the other departments.

The channels for the product must also be defined and marketing must be certain that those channels are prepared to sell the product effectively.

Last but not least, marketing must set the appropriate price for the product.

Developing Expectations—Three Areas

Because a business should always be adapting to an ever-changing external environment, the internal environment will likely also be in flux. Since it is marketing that defines the ways in which the firm must change in order to be in tune with the external environment, marketing can be expected to also give notice of reflected internal change.

The first expectation that needs to be constantly reflected into the organization at large is the state of and expected changes in the external environment. This sharing of knowledge:

1) educates everyone regarding the context of his or her own job and will thus facilitate better individual decisions.

2) reflects the turf of the common battle and will thus foster cooperation and understanding.

3) helps prevent surprises and conflict concerning the necessary actions to be taken.

If marketing is doing its *Understand* and *Predict* jobs well, it has a long-term view of the financial structure of firms in the market, and it knows how the future will be different from the current financial structure. This is a vitally important expectation to report to top and financial management because it is the most closely-watched set of guidelines used by shareholders, and other interested parties outside the company. If margins, or return on investment, or inventory status, for example, are going to change, you and your management must be prepared.

The other expectation that marketing can nurture in the internal environment concerns systems and human skills that will be necessary. If the number or percentage of people with particular skills is going to change, or systems within the company need to be altered or added, then planning for those changes must begin.

Developing Investments—Seven Items

In addition to new products, many other changes may be necessary in order for the firm to be successful in the world to come. The company as a whole must be in tune with the environment, meaning that its constituent parts must also be in tune. That often takes money. Money represents investments, and it is the job of marketing to set expectations about investments which will be necessary.

Any area of the firm may require an investment, but the areas that most often require them are: product promotion, research and development, sales, manufacturing, operations, management information systems, and, of course, marketing itself. The role of marketing here is the same as it plays in developing products—an active partnership. Marketing does not have the technical expertise to make the necessary changes in these areas, but it knows what the firm must do in order to be successful.

Developing Organizational Structure—Six Areas

The same marketing expertise that knows which products to develop and what investments to make within the firm, also knows if the structure of the firm should be changed. Perhaps a decentralized Research & Development department would be more in tune with tomorrow's market requirements; maybe combining two Management Information Service areas, or changing the structure of the sales force. These organizational structure expectations, or success requirements, must be expressed to management.

Marketing is not, of course, the sole determiner of organizational structure, but, in its role as discoverer and keeper of the firm's success requirements, it needs to be a strong voice. All functional areas: marketing, sales, research and development, manufacturing, operations, and management information service, should receive consideration.

The Develop Formula

Develop Products
Product requirements
Service requirements
Terms and conditions
Support requirements
Distribution outlets
Time frames
Price
Develop Expectations
Environmental
Financial
Skills and Systems
Develop Investments
Promotional
Research and Development
Sales
Manufacturing
Operations
Management Information Services
Marketing
Developing Organizational Structure
Marketing
Sales
Research and Development
Manufacturing
Operations
Management Information Services

Chapter 6

The Promote Formula

Now that you understand the context in which you are trying to make a profit, can predict the environment, have appropriate products to offer as well as an organizational structure to support the products and their sales—now you get to the aspect of marketing that many people mistakenly believe to be its only job—promotion.

The sales force does the actual selling, the day to day interacting with prospects and customers. They must be backed up, not just with the knowledge and structure that is the result of *Understanding*, *Predicting*, and *Developing*, but with active day-to-day promotional activities. That is the job of marketing.

There are four things to promote: the products, the company, sales to prospects, and partnerships with customers.

Promoting the Products—Ten Ways

There are ten ways that are almost always used to promote products. Others ways may be applicable or peculiar to your products, and some of these ten may not apply, but they require consideration.

Media advertising is the first. It reaches a great many people at a low unit cost and establishes presence in the mind of prospects. Its dollar cost can be expensive, though, and its results can be erratic.

Either a product lends itself to media advertising or it doesn't. If it does and the results of advertising are bad, the fault is in the advertisements. If it doesn't, the results from advertising will never be good. Products with broad diversified prospects lend themselves to media advertising (we are not here discussing company advertising, but product advertising).

Assuming a product does appeal to a large base of prospects, then advertisments will fail because:

1)   the ads themselves are not effective,

2)   the media is not appropriate, or

3)   some number of advertisements were run instead of a campaign - advertisements do not work, only advertising campaigns work.

Despite the continuing propagation of advertising styles and techniques, a great deal of research has been done to determine what really works in this field. This information is widely available and just as widely ignored; most advertisements you see violate the known effectiveness rules. Marketing professionals—who must approve advertisements—have only themselves to blame for ignorance of these rules and should make a point of learning them.

Appropriate media selection has become easier with all of the computerized data now available from the media vendors. It requires patience and skeptical analysis, but effective choices can be made.

And the solution to the ineffectiveness of small numbers of advertisments is clear, do not budget or run advertisements until you can afford and justify an entire campaign.

This is not a book on the causes or cures for the abysmal state of advertising effectiveness. (However, to get a taste of the former, and a vigorous dose of the latter, read *Olgilvy on Advertising* by David Olgilvy.) The point, as far as this book is concerned, is that media advertising is a powerful tool and must be considered.

Direct mail is another powerful tool. It can zero in on prospects and lends itself well to specific audiences. List selection is highly variable and can be selected so as to reach almost any conceivable group of people. You will need to pay a great deal of attention to the design and text of the direct mail piece. Again, the rules are well-known for what works and what does not in this medium, and consultation with a professional in this field is recommended.

Press releases are an easy form of free publicity. An up-to-date list of the magazines that service your market should be maintained and a press release about a new product, product enhancement, an application for the product, or anything else should go out every month like clockwork, regardless of your product or specific market.

Collateral literature such as data sheets, brochures and pamphlets are necessary and self-evident promotional tools.

Application information is often a very powerful sales tool. This can take the form of application notes for technical products, recipe booklets for food products, and educational literature for just about any product area.

Product documentation, manuals, instructions, and so on, are often overlooked as a source of promotion. Making them easy to use will result in more recommendations for your product. Using the documentation to continue selling the product is an important function - you want the customer to buy again or recommend the product to others. In addition, the documentation itself is often a powerful piece of collateral literature, particularly with technical audiences.

Trade shows are another useful promotional tool, sometimes. Companies often exhibit at them only because *everyone else is there*, or out of mindless tradition, but they can serve a useful function. It is up to you to devise valid promotion alternatives and determine if they are useful to your situation.

Catalogs are powerful tools in some markets. If your products or market lends itself to catalog sales or promotion, consider using them.

Articles in magazines by a member of your company are persuasive— and free—promotional tools. You are advised to get acquainted with the editors of magazines that service your market, discuss their editorial needs with them, and fill those needs with articles based on your products. Except in the consumer magazines, there is usually more magazine space available than good articles.

The people who sell your product, the sales force, will benefit from education and competitive information regarding the product. Sales guides, which cover product applications, competition, prospect profiles, and so on, are valuable tools for marketing to provide.

Promoting the Company—Seven Areas

People often buy a product partly, or even solely, on the strength of the manufacturer's reputation. As a rule, promoting the company is as important as promoting the products and is usually less expensive.

Start with media relations. Just getting acquainted with the editors and writers that service your market's media is an important step. You will be called for quotes and mentioned more frequently and favorably than if you are not known, in which case you will, of course, not be quoted or mentioned at all.

Press releases regarding the company, like product press releases, should go out regularly to the media.

Articles about the company have an appropriate place, perhaps in a different sort of vehicle than articles about products or technology, perhaps a business vehicle instead of a product one. Cultivate relationships with editors in the appropriate media to see when they can use such articles.

Sponsorships of public, customer or trade events or publications can be valuable and should be evaluated.

The company should also be advertised. This is often called image advertising, and when properly done, is a very powerful tool. This may or may not be appropriate for your situation but it is one of the actions that must be considered.

Any publicly-held company cannot afford to be without some kind of investor relations program. Managing the relationship of the company with its owners is a job for management, but the content of the investor relations effort reaches a far broader audience than simply the shareholders and creditors. Your customers and prospects also pay close attention to this information. It therefore behooves marketing to become involved in the investor relations effort.

Newsletters or company magazines are often an effective way to keep your company in the minds of customers and prospects and keep them informed about your products. They establish your company as a classy, knowledgeable, and helpful vendor.

Promoting Sales to Prospects—Two Ways

While the day-to-day efforts of selling the products are done by the sales force, there are two common ways that marketing gets involved in closing sales: presentations and seminars.

As the repository of all the knowledge gained in the *Understand* and *Predict* stages of their job, the marketing staff is often more of an expert than the salesperson on the product and the broader needs of the prospect. In addition, if the sales force handles many products, they simply cannot be expert on all of them. So when a presentation is called for, marketing is often the logical organization to do it. This means that marketing must have prepared both the content of the presentations (which will usually require only slight customizing for delivery to any specific prospect) and the delivery vehicle, (e.g. slides, video tapes, overheads, scripts). Even if the sales force is designated to give the presentations, it is the job of marketing to prepare them and have them on hand. Ahead of time. As a matter of course.

Seminars are basically in-depth presentations with a greater breadth or technical scope. This is your chance to sell prospects with your knowledge, their need for your product, and also their broader concerns and business issues and an opportunity to place your product within that context. All the information gathered in the *Understand* and *Predict* exercises can be used here.

Unless you are in a custom product business, you hope to sell more than one of any product. It follows that the various customers for this product will share needs and broader issues. Therefore, a great deal of the seminar content and delivery vehicles can be prepared ahead of time, and later customized to the specific prospect. This is a routine job of marketing.

Promoting Customer Partnerships—Two Areas

In very few areas do you want to sell a product to customers and forget about them. Most often, you would like them to be repeat customers. In any case, many of the best ideas for future products come from your existing customers.

Therefore, routine communication with your customers is an important job of marketing. Here you will hear about product problems, product suggestions, and customer needs, and get ideas as to the best ways to solve these problems. You will also learn which direction your product development efforts should take. Building a system and structure to make this kind of communication happen is a very important job of marketing.

In addition, your customers will usually want to know about your future product directions. Since your products are incorporated into their products or consumption pattern, knowing your plans helps them with their own planning. Sharing these plans with trusted customers is also a source of feedback and will help you stay on a market-directed course during development. In addition, this information sharing also functions as an initial sales call for the new product.

It is a vital job of marketing to create a structure and system to make this two way communication happen.

The Promote Formula

Promoting the Products
Media advertising
Direct mail
Press releases
Collateral literature
Application information
Documentation
Trade shows
Catalogs
Articles
Sales guides
Promoting the Company
Media relations
Press releases
Articles
Sponsorships
Advertising
Investor relations
Newsletters/Magazines
Promoting Sales to Prospects
Presentations
Seminars
Promoting Customer Partnerships
Communication
Future directions

Part Three

The Marketing Planning Formula

Chapter 7

The Identify Opportunities Formula

As indicated in Part One, the major marketing planning tasks are to Identify Opportunities, Set Objectives, Develop Strategy, Formulate Plans, and Implement and Control the important elements of those plans. This section will follow the general outline of strategic marketing activities defined by Phillip Kotler in his book, *Marketing Management: Analysis, Planning and Control* (1976, Prentice-Hall), although we will modify many of the particulars of the model he suggests. In this chapter we will examine the ways to analyze market opportunities and provide a formula to cover the 90% of these planning activities that can be done routinely.

Environmental vs. Company Opportunities

It is important first to distinguish between environmental opportunities and company opportunities. The environment is usually full of opportunities. The *Understand* and *Predict* functions will have revealed a world full of needs and potential profitable ventures. But only a few of those environmental opportunities represent a company opportunity.

Company opportunities are instances of environmental opportunities wherin the company enjoys a *differential* advantage by virtue of a distinctive competence. That is, the things that the company can do well match the requirements of an environmental opportunity.

For example, computer companies tend to have a distinctive competence in the software area and enjoy a differential advantage regarding opportunities in the software market. Likewise, automobile manufacturers tend to have a differential advantage regarding environmental opportunities to provide transportation. But a differential advantage is not always tied to the company's main line of business. An automobile manufacturer may have a distinctive competence in producing certain kinds of manufacturing software and may thus enjoy a differential advantage in that seemingly unrelated market.

To identify opportunities, a company must distill the information from the *Understand* and *Predict* functions to see where its distinctive abilities align with the requirements of environmental opportunities, yielding a differential advantage and a company opportunity.

The discussions that follow are mainly concerned with company opportunities that relate to the firm's main line of business, but, as we saw above, differential advantages and company opportunities may be present in other areas as well. Ferreting out these other opportunities is one of the marketing tasks that fall partly within the 10% of non-routine activities.

Identify Product/Market Opportunities—Three Areas

The first of three sets of company opportunities tend to be based on either product opportunities or market opportunities, or both. Figure 7-1 below outlines the three major types of product/market opportunities that center around existing products or markets. The figure also shows a second major set of opportunities (diversification opportunities discussed in the next section) that is concerned with new products for new markets.

	Present Products	New Products
Present Markets	Market Penetration	Product Development
New Markets	Market Development	Diversification

Figure 7-1

Product/market opportunities are of three kinds:

Market penetration can be an opportunity when the company's products have not exhausted the existing potential market share. Unless the market for your product has been saturated, this is usually a viable opportunity.

Market development can be an opportunity when the company's products have appeal to markets other than those presently being serviced. This kind of opportunity takes advantage of the company's name recognition in the new market and your understanding of the needs of that market.

Product development can be an opportunity when the company's present markets have need of additional products related to those they are already buying. This opportunity is usually exploited by product-line extensions and product enhancements.

The product/market opportunities: market penetration, market development, and product development, are sometimes called intensive growth opportunities, since either the existing product set or existing market is exploited (grown) further.

You must analyze the environmental opportunities derived from the *Understand* and *Predict* data and see if there is a product/market company opportunity. Intensive growth opportunities are the most common opportunities to arise, and, unless you are in a declining industry, it would be unusual for one or more of them not to be appropriate.

Identify Diversification Opportunities—Three Ways

The second most common kind of opportunities is providing new products to new markets. Diversification opportunities also come in three variants:

Concentric diversification describes an opportunity when new but related products can be developed for new markets.

Horizontal diversification describes an opportunity when unrelated products can be developed for new markets within existing customers.

Conglomerate diversification represents an opportunity when unrelated products can be added to serve unrelated markets, and is usually undertaken to offset a deficiency or undesirable cyclicness of the present line of business.

It is likely that there are several diversification opportunities that may be appropriate for your business in the sea of environmental opportunities.

Identify Integrative Opportunities—Three Kinds

The third major set of opportunities do not relate to a product/market configuration, but to the addition of some facet of the production process to your operations. Integrative growth can represent an opportunity when it is profitable for the company to integrate its operation with suppliers, customers, or competitors.

Backward integration can be an opportunity when it is viable to assume control of a supplier.

Forward integration is an opportunity when it becomes profitable for a company to gain control over its means of distribution.

Horizontal integration is an opportunity when it makes sense to obtain control of a competitor.

One or several of these kinds of opportunities will become apparent upon a careful analysis of the information provided by the *Understand* and *Predict* functions, and they must all be considered.

The Identify Opportunities Formula

Identify Product/Market Opportunities
Market development
Product development
Market penetration
Identify Diversification Opportunities
Concentric
Horizontal
Conglomerate
Identify Integrative Opportunities
Backward
Forward
Horizontal

Chapter 8

The Set Objectives Formula

Now that company opportunities are identified, a chain of events must be set into motion to exploit them. The first step in this chain is to *Set Objectives*, to state those things you wish to accomplish. Objectives serve the same function as a destination on a trip—they provide a goal and a constant point at which to aim. Just as you would not start a trip without knowing where you were going, you cannot productively engage in marketing activities without clearly knowing what you want to accomplish.

Objectives must meet certain environmental constraints and internal requirements.

Set Objectives to Environmental Constraints—Two Areas

The objectives must be to support a company opportunity. Goals not designed to exploit an opportunity contribute nothing to the ultimate corporate mission, which is to make a profit.

Objectives must be measurable. Otherwise there is no way to tell if they have been reached, or what progress is being made toward reaching them. Not all things are precisely measurable; customer satisfaction, for instance, will always be a bit intangible, but this does not excuse management from insisting on the best measure possible. In fact, all statements of objectives should include the measurement criteria in them; e.g., increase customer satisfaction with product X - as measured by the number of defective returns.

Set Objectives to Internal Requirements—Four Concerns

Objectives must be specific. *Increase market share* is not good enough. You must state by how much you want to increase it, and when.

They must be realistic. Pie-in-the-sky wishes do not qualify as legitimate objectives.

They must be manageable. Management attention must be able to direct them and to track their progress. The optimum number of objectives is usually eight or less.

They must be consistent. They cannot contradict each other, nor can the actions necessary for their implementation be in conflict.

The Set Objectives Formula

Set Objectives to Environmental Constraints
Support a company opportunity
Measurable
Set Objectives to Internal Requirements
Specific
Realistic
Manageable
Consistent

Chapter 9

The Develop Strategy Formula

Now that you have identified marketing opportunities and set objectives, you must start to detail how to accomplish those objectives. This detailing is done in two steps: Developing Strategy and Formulating Plans. While the objectives state the goals, strategy statements outline how to get to those goals.

Each objective is supported by strategies and each strategy has supporting plans. It is important to remember that all strategies, like objectives, must be measurable and specific, and where applicable, quantified.

The elements of marketing strategy unfold around the central concept of marketing opportunities—that all opportunities consist of some product being sold to some market.

Develop Target Market Strategy—Six Areas

The first element of marketing strategy is to identify the target market for the product. This may be one of the market segments identified in the *Understand* activity or some combination thereof, or the target market may be some unique mix of previously identified segments. While the target market may have been already loosely identified when *Identifying Opportunities*, it must now be delineated clearly and in detail. The target market must be large enough and growing fast enough to accomplish your objective. It must be available, and it must have unsatisfied needs that your product can fulfill.

Develop Market Entry Strategy—Three Considerations

The second element of marketing strategy is to determine the method of entry into the target market. This is usually accomplished in one of three ways: by acquisition of a company or product, by product or market development, or by collaboration with another firm.

Develop Product Positioning Strategy—Four Elements

The third element of marketing strategy is to position the product in the target market. This activity is usually defined as prescribing the *four P's* of the marketing mix. The *four P's* are product, place, promotion, and price.

Product refers to the product attributes; they must be broadly defined. The detailed definition of the product's attributes is done in the *Develop* phase of marketing operations; but the general attributes must be decided on here in *Product Positioning Strategy*. The product's features must be defined in broad brush, including packaging, service, and any of its other important attributes.

Defining place means to define the broad scheme of distribution for the product. Again, the detailed implementation of distribution channels is reserved for the *Develop* function of marketing operations, but the important aspects of distribution must be stated here. These may include the type of channel, channel coverage, channel conflict resolutions, and so on.

The day-to-day activities of product promotion are the concern of the *Promote* function of marketing operations, but the broad attributes of the campaign should be formulated here. Important aspects of advertising, selling, publicity, and so on, need to be delineated.

The important aspects of price should also be decided now. These may include price levels, discount policies, etc.

Develop Timing Strategy—Two Items

All activities occur at some time and over some schedule. Critical dates and linkages among the elements of the marketing strategies must be clearly stated and conflicts removed.

The Develop Strategy Formula

Develop Target Market Strategy
Map to existing segments
Map to new segments
Large enough
Growing fast enough
Available
Unsatisfied needs
Develop Market Entry Strategy
Acquire
Develop
Collaborate
Develop Product Positioning Strategy
Product
Place
Promotion
Price
Develop Timing Strategy
Dates
Linkages

Chapter 10

The Formulate Plans Formula

Plans are the detailed statements of activities to be done. They are the blueprints by which management will measure the progress of marketing activities. Like objectives and strategies, plans must be composed of specific, measurable, quantified statements.

The first job is to add detail to the strategies concerning market entry.

Formulate Market Entry Plans—Three Plans

The set of activities and milestones concerning acquisition, development, or collaboration must all be defined and passed over to the operational *Develop* area within marketing. These include all of the relevant names, dates and numbers.

Formulate Product Positioning Plans—Four Attributes

The set of activities and goals concerning product attributes, distribution activities, promotional campaigns and price elements must be defined and also passed over to the *Develop and Promote* functions. These include sales targets, promotional guidelines, price schedule parameters, and all of the relevant product attributes.

Set Marketing Budgets—Four Areas

The second element of *Formulating Plans* is to set the marketing budgets. Everything costs money, and by setting budgets you are defining how much of an activity will be completed. Doing the activities is a concern of the tactical marketing operations who must implement the plans; but what and how much is completed is defined by the marketing plans and budgets.

The total marketing budget must be determined, and the amount allocated to each marketing operational area and each marketing planning area must be broken out.

The budget must also be allocated between products.

Formulate Plans Formula

Formulate Market Entry Plans
Acquisition
Development
Collaboration
Formulate Product Positioning Plans
Product
Place
Promotion
Price
Set Budgets
Total marketing budget
Allocation to operational activities
Allocation to planning activities
Allocation among products

Chapter 11

The Implement and Control Formula

The final job of marketing planning is to *Implement and Control* the plans. In general, the implementation of the plans is done by giving direction to the *Develop and Promote* marketing operations groups. Controlling the plans is the primary activity in this area and is an ongoing task accomplished through three primary mechanisms: Plan Reviews, Budget Reviews, and Strategy Calibration

Plan Reviews—Two Kinds

The plans drawn up for market entry and product positioning were specific, measurable and quantified, for a reason. With concrete plans, actual progress can be measured. It is important to regularly review the progress of the implementation against the plans themselves. This is often done quarterly, but the right frequency is that which does not allow the implementation of the plans to deviate far from their dates and milestones without being noticed. At these reviews the progress against plans should be monitored and corrective action taken as necessary.

It is important to understand the reasons for any deviation from the plans. Reasons such as human ineffectiveness or resource misallocation can be corrected to keep the implementation on track. But it may be the case that the plans themselves are unrealistic and need to be changed.

If a plan is unrealistic, so may be the strategy that it supports, and the strategy may need to be altered. Likewise, the objective that the strategy supports may also be unrealistic and need revision. And the opportunity that the strategy attempts to exploit may be unobtainable and need revision. The regular *Plan Review* therefore functions not only to monitor and control the implementation of the plans, but as a check and feedback loop to the viability of the opportunities and their objectives, strategies and plans.

Budget Reviews—Four Areas

In addition to financial controls that budget reviews represent, they also serve to monitor the implementation of the marketing plans. Budget reviews survey the implementation activities from a cash flow point of view rather than a date and milestone viewpoint. Also, discrepancies between plans and their implementation can escape plan reviews, but may show up on budget reviews.

Activities over-budget may require corrective action or a revision of the plans to bring them in line with available monies. Activities under-budget may not be moving ahead fast enough to meet plans or may represent additional funds available to other activities.

Budget reviews need to encompass the total marketing budget, the marketing operations budget (by major activity), the marketing planning budget (by major activity), and the marketing budget by products.

Strategy Calibration—Three Types

Strategy calibration is a tool of strategic marketing used to quickly gauge whether the entire structure of marketing opportunities, objectives, strategies and plans is in tune with the constantly changing environment. It consists of identifying bellwether variables in the environment that track or foreshadow the state of the market, the opportunities, and the competition. Updated and reviewed regularly, these calibration variables provide a quick, intuitive check on the soundness of the company's strategic marketing structure.

For example, sales in a targeted market may be a calibrating variable for a market penetration strategy. Major sales in the industry could be a calibration variable for the state of competitors' momentum. Company recognition surveys may be a calibration variable for a company attempting to gain exposure in a market.

The set of variables that perform the function of strategy calibration will differ from industry to industry; within an industry from company to company; and from year to year. There is no formula for what the calibration variables are, but strategy calibration is surely something that is valuable to do. Indeed, it is constantly done informally inside of most peoples' minds. Doing it formally will insure that the calibration variables are, if not universally agreed upon, at least universally understood, and that the resulting picture of the market, the opportunities, and the competition is widely shared.

The Implement and Control Formula

Plan Reviews
Market entry plans
Product positioning plans
Budget Reviews
Total budgets
Operations budgets
Planning budgets
Product budgets
Strategy Calibration
Market calibration
Opportunity calibration
Competitor calibration

Part Four

The Marketing Formula

The Marketing Formula

The previous five chapters have outlined the marketing planning process and activities. These activities, when combined with the marketing operations activities described in Part 1, constitute the predictable tasks of marketing.

Not every task can be done completely all of the time. Circumstances may dictate that some tasks be omitted or combined, or done in only a cursory manner, or may call for tasks not in the formulas. We will examine some of these situations in the following chapters. But with these formulas as a guide, those kinds of decisions can be made with full awareness of deviations from the ideal rules of marketing.

The Understand Formula

Understand the Market	Understand the Competitors
Size by sales	Defining characteristics
Size by units	Channels
Size by profits	Sales procedures
Super-market size by sales	Terms and conditions
Super-market size by units	Services
Competitors by sales	Product set
Competitors by units	Product strategies
Competitors by profits	Profit Margins
Customer type by sales	Customers-who
Customer type by units	Customers-why
Customer type by profits	Promotional tactics
Geography by sales	Marketing strengths
Geography by units	Sales strengths
Geography by profits	Financial strengths
Channels by sales	Manufacturing strengths
Channels by units	Technical strengths
Channels by profits	Marketing weaknesses
Specific segmentations by sales	Sales weaknesses
Specific segmentations by units	Financial weaknesses
Specific segmentations by profits	Manufacturing weaknesses
Technological influences	Technical weaknesses
Manufacturing influences	
Other influences	
Financial influences	

Understand the Customer	Understand the Products
Define existing customers	Competing products
Define potential customers	Product categories
Product type buying criteria	Why used
Vendor criteria	Substitutes
Buying patterns	Life cycle stage
Decision makers	Relation to other products
Decision process	Percentage of cost
Product use	How the product works
Sales and lost sales analysis	

The Predict Formula

Predict The Market	Predict The Competitors
Size by sales	Defining characteristics
Size by units	Channels
Size by profits	Sales procedures
Super-market size by sales	Terms and conditions
Super-market size by units	Services
Competitors by sales	Product set
Competitors by units	Product strategies
Competitors by profits	Profit margins
Customer type by sales	Customers-who
Customer type by units	Customers-why
Customer type by profits	Promotional tactics
Geography by sales	Marketing strengths
Geography by units	Sales strengths
Geography by profits	Financial strengths
Channels by sales	Manufacturing strengths
Channels by units	Technical strengths
Channels by profits	Marketing weaknesses
Specific segmentations by sales	Sales weaknesses
Specific segmentations by units	Financial weaknesses
Specific segmentations by profits	Manufacturing weaknesses
Technological influences	Technical weaknesses
Manufacturing influences	
Other influences	
Financial influences	
Predict the Customer	**Predict the Products**
Future customers	Competing products
Potential customers	product categories
Product buying criteria	why used
Vendor criteria	Substitutes
Buying patterns	Life cycle stage
Decision makers	Relation to other products
Decision process	Percentage of cost
Product use	How the product works
Sales and lost sales analysis	

The Develop Formula

Develop Products
Product requirements
Service requirements
Terms and conditions
Support requirements
Distribution outlets
Time frames
Price
Develop Expectations
Environmental
Financial
Skills and Systems
Develop Investments
Promotional
Research and Development
Sales
Manufacturing
Operations
Management Information Services
Marketing
Developing Organizational Structure
Marketing
Sales
Research and Development
Manufacturing
Operations
Management Information Services

The Promote Formula

Promoting the Products
Media advertising
Direct mail
Press releases
Collateral literature
Application information
Documentation
Trade shows
Catalogs
Articles
Sales guides
Promoting the Company
Media relations
Press releases
Articles
Sponsorships
Advertising
Investor relations
Newsletters/Magazines
Promoting Sales to Prospects
Presentations
Seminars
Promoting Customer Partnerships
Communication
Future directions

The Identify Opportunities Formula

Identify Product/Market Opportunities
Market development
Product development
Market penetration
Identify Diversification Opportunities
Concentric
Horizontal
Conglomerate
Identify Integrative Opportunities
Backward
Forward
Horizontal

The Set Objectives Formula

Set Objectives to Environmental Constraints
Support a company opportunity
Measurable
Set Objectives to Internal Requirements
Specific
Realistic
Manageable
Consistent

The Develop Strategy Formula

Develop Target Market Strategy
Map to existing segments
Map to new segments
Large enough
Growing fast enough
Available
Unsatisfied needs
Develop Market Entry Strategy
Acquire
Develop
Collaborate
Develop Product Positioning Strategy
Product
Place
Promotion
Price
Develop Timing Strategy
Dates
Linkages

Forrmulate Plans Formula

Formulate Market Entry Plans
Acquisition
Development
Collaboration
Formulate Product Positioning Plans
Product
Place
Promotion
Price
Set Budgets
Total marketing budget
Allocation to operational activities
Allocation to planning activities
Allocation among products

The Implement and Control Formula

Plan Reviews
Market entry plans
Product positioning plans
Budget Reviews
Total budgets
Operations budgets
Planning budgets
Product budgets
Strategy Calibration
Market calibration
Opportunity calibration
Competitor calibration

The seven pages containing *The Market Formula* may be copied or reproduced without further permission.

Part Five

Putting the Formula to Work

Chapter 12

Putting the Formula to Work
in the Organization

The formulas presented in the preceding chapters described individual marketing activities. The model presented in Chapter 2 defined the relationships between the activities. Now it is a matter of doing the activities, and ordering them according to the model. You now have a marketing blueprint to follow that will insure that no valuable activity is overlooked, and that individual activities are coordinated. How the Marketing Formula is used by various organizational groups is examined in this chapter.

Putting the formula to work in the organization.

Any organized scheme for a complex human activity immediately suggests an organizational structure. Corporate and marketing management should evaluate how well their present organizational structure supports the performance of the distinct marketing duties set forth by the comprehensive model.

Indeed, the comprehensive model presented here, separating planning and operations activities, suggests separate planning and operations organizations within the marketing function (obviously this is implied only for organizations sufficiently large to support such a diversified structure). The operations organization would be charged with performing marketing tasks, and the planning organization with determining direction and content of the activities.

An operations organization would own the tasks of *Understand* and *Predict* the environment; centered around market, customer, and environmental research. The operations group would also manage the *Develop* functions of marketing, classically centering around product and project management. And the operations organization would manage the traditional operational promotional activities.

The marketing planning organization is to be charged with using the information gathered by the *Understand* and *Predict* groups in order to *Set Objectives* for products and markets, *Develop Strategies* and *Formulate Plans* to achieve the objectives, give direction to the operational *Develop* and *Promote* groups, and devise means of maintaining planning Control.

This organization of duties is similar to that often found in industry. However, the model presented here, with its clear delineation of the various operational and planning activities and its definition of the relationships between the activities, should help avoid some common problems.

These problems can take the form of: confusion about the distinction between operational marketing and marketing planning, boundary disputes between marketing organizations, overlapping responsibilities between groups, poor coordination of marketing areas, and incomplete marketing activity coverage.

In addition, with marketing activities organized around a general model of the marketing function, a practical degree of stability is brought to marketing activities. The marketing organization can evolve in pace with the market or corporation, rather than gyrate wildly with each successive manager or product.

Putting the Formula to Work for Marketing Management

The flow of information between the elements of the model indicate relationships between the marketing organizations. A reporting chain, information system, or organizational structure that prevents these information flows between groups will result in a disjointed, uncoordinated marketing effort. I suggest that marketing managers examine the structure of information flow within their organizations—with respect to the model—and correct impediments to efficiency.

Using the formulas makes it possible to assign a manager to well-defined marketing responsibilities, which allows the matching of a person's skills and interests with the requirements of a particular position. Instead of hoping that a marketing manager *has what it takes* for a particular job, it is possible to evaluate what it takes and make an appropriate personnel decision. For instance, the model's delineation of the differences between marketing operations and marketing planning should make it clear that someone who has done a great job in an operations area, such as *Develop* products, may not necessarily have the skills for planning jobs such as *Set Objectives*, and vice versa. Just as we have come to understand that sales skills do not necessarily indicate marketing skills, we can now see that not all marketing skills are the same.

Putting the Formula to Work for Corporate Management

With the separate elements of marketing and their inter-relationships clearly defined, it is possible to manage marketing as a set of systematic activities: to monitor the critical marketing activities, to diagnose problems within the marketing organization, and to align marketing effectively with other functional organizations.

General managers should consider evaluating their present marketing elements to determine if bringing them more in line with the model would be an effective arrangement. In addition, since the internal activities of the marketing function are made clear by the formulas, general management has a yardstick by which to measure marketing—namely, how well are each of the marketing activities being performed and how well are they coordinated?

Putting the Formula to Work for the Individual

The model can help marketing people modify their behavior as a result of answering the following questions:

- Am I (is my organization) addressing all of the activities necessary to do my job completely and correctly?
- Do I (does my organization) have the right communication channels in place with other areas in marketing, and other functions within the firm?
- Am I (is my organization) getting the right information from other people and organizations within marketing and other functions in the firm?
- Am I (is my organization) giving appropriate and useful information to the other marketing areas and other functional areas that depend on my information to do their job?

The Cost of Implementing the Model and Using the Formulas

Implementing this model is not expensive. Since it addresses only the organization and completeness of what are probably existing activities, it should not require large expenditures.

Implementing this model is not painful. Most organizations already perform most of the activities outlined in the formulas. What is probably necessary is some reorganization of the activities. Individual people may need to be reassigned, but neither the model nor the formulas should obviate the need for existing marketing skills.

The implementation of this model and use of the formulas may require different reporting structures and different inter-group dependencies than presently exist. This may cause some friction within the present marketing structure, but, on the whole, any changes would probably not be so radical as to cause major upheaval, and in any case, the changes can be implemented at an acceptable speed.

Chapter 13

Putting the Formula to Work in Structural Situations

I have mentioned several times that the formulas presented in this book are complete marketing formulas; they list all of the aspects of the function. It may not be possible or desirable to do all of them in detail, all of the time. The possibility and desirability of doing certain activities will vary by the structural situation of the organization. A mature consumer goods company, for example, will have a far different marketing activity mix from that of a high technology start-up.

How you use the *Marketing Formula* is a question of how you select, disregard, or slant the activities in the entire formula. You must determine how many of the activities in the *Marketing Formula* are appropriate for your situation, and in how much depth you need to do them. We'll take a look at some of the more common distinguishing characteristics of structural situations to give you an idea how the marketing formula might be used in them.

Putting the Formula to Work in a Large Company

On one hand, a large organization is the best place to implement the marketing formula—to implement all of the marketing activities discussed here. Most of the activities are probably already being done in some fashion, and a large company certainly has the resources to fund all of them. Moreover, the larger the company, the less it can get by on incomplete marketing efforts and niche market sales and the more it needs to have an extensive and complete marketing operation.

On the other hand, a large organization has probably organized these marketing activities in a less than fully efficient manner. They are probably spread out over several internal marketing organizations that may not communicate with each other, or with other groups in the company as effectively as they could. In addition, the delineation of marketing tasks between these groups is probably confused. While obtaining funding for marketing activities may not be a problem in large organizations, changing an organizational *power* structure—even to improve it—is often difficult.

The challenge in large organizations is to implement the entire *Marketing Formula*. It is usually possible to get funding for activities that are demonstrably beneficial. Indeed, it is possible that too much is already being done, resulting in overlapping responsibilities between marketing groups, duplication of effort, and inefficient expenditures of money. The challenge is to align the structure of the organization so that the tasks are done efficiently and the communication flows outlined by the model are facilitated, encouraged, and evaluated.

For large companies, I suggest that marketing and general management conduct an audit to determine which marketing activities are being provided by various marketing groups. Who receives the information generated by these groups? Who acts on the information?. The next step is to see if the structure of the organization cannot be gradually re-shaped to be more in line with the model presented in Chapter 2. As that structure comes into place, the responsibilities of the groups within it can be assigned the appropriate parts of the *Marketing Formula*. This can be done for the entire corporation, or for a part of it.

None of these changes is easy. In a large organization, in fact in any kind of human environment, the challenging of people's power bases is very difficult. But the focus of this book is not on how to fight political battles but on which marketing activities should be incorporated into a company. The successful achievement of the right marketing structure will always depend on the visionary leadership of strong managers.

Putting the Formula to Work in a Small Company

The problem in small companies is often one of either resources—there are not enough people to do a complete job of marketing (which translates into not enough money to hire them), or one of lack of structure—or the job gets done but in a disorganized manner, or both.

The first step I suggest for small concerns is that they go through the *Marketing Formula*, selecting each task that is presently done and writing beside it the name of the person who does it. Then, next to each task that is passively done (i.e., it is done intuitively and the information obtained from it is probably never written down) and write down the name of the person who does it, with a note that it is done passively.

The second step for small company managers is to go through the model and the *Marketing Formula* and note: 1. which activities and communication flows must happen in order for the organization to continue to exist; 2. which must happen in order to increase profits and/or growth; 3. which are not necessary for their particular situation. Marketing activities may fall into any of these three categories, and where they fall is entirely dependent on the company.

Now do a comparison of the results of the first and second step, and take corrective action to make them alike. One of three things will be necessary: either people's present activities can be brought into line with the desired state, or more people will have to be hired, or both. If you feel you can't afford to hire more people, remember that marketing is a significant investment for a small company hoping to grow. The marketing expenditures necessary for small companies to succeed and grow is often a greater percentage of revenues than it is for a large company.

Small companies are most likely to concentrate marketing planning in the hands of one or a few people; the result is that the formality and explicitness of the planning is often neglected. I do not want to suggest that the process must be more formal—the beauty and competitive advantage of small companies is their flexibility—but I do mean to say that it should always be explicit. The purpose of planning is to set direction for the company and control it's movement towards the destination. Companies are always, and will always be in some state; i.e, some position of profitability, size, market share, customer base, etc. Either the company's efforts are directed toward bringing the company to a desired state or the company will wander without direction to some random state.

The writing down of a plan is a wonderfully rigorous activity. It forces the setting of goals which are often missed in small concerns. Without goals companies float without direction. Writing down a plan forces logical planning and connection of all the steps necessary to reach goals. This does not require the hiring of a staff or necessarily the expenditure of money. It merely requires a bit of time and thought.

For small companies, I suggest that making marketing planning explicit is perhaps the most important marketing activity they can undertake. It takes away assumptions that have been made erroneously and exposes them to evaluation. It forces the choice of corporate destination. It requires the formation of workable plans to reach the destination.

Putting the Formula to Work in the Technology Company

Technology companies are those that use new technologies to produce entirely new kinds of products. They are sometimes referred to as *supply driven*, as opposed to *demand driven* companies. It is said that their new products create their own market. For example, there was no market for, indeed no awareness of, computers before their commercial introduction in the 1950s. This situation clearly differs from demand-driven industries where products are manufactured to meet an existing product demand.

With regard to these new technology products, there are often no direct competitors or competing products, no awareness on the part of potential customers of the capabilities of the product and consequently no demand for that particular product.

However, these new products were designed to accomplish some task, to meet some need. And potential customers are certainly well enough aware of their needs. They may not have ever heard of a computer in the fifties but they certainly could appreciate the ability to speed up bookkeeping tasks. Remember, customers do not buy products, they buy what the product does - not computers but computational ability, not genetically engineered drugs but relief from disease.

Therefore, the technology company will often redefine the parts of the *Marketing Formula* that are concerned with competition to mean competition from substitute products and the current means of accomplishing the same task. Other than that semantic distinction, the *Marketing Formula* applies in full.

In technology companies, there is often a difference in emphasis regarding the method for formulating new ideas culminating in new products. Since the technology company, by definition, fulfills customer desires through the application of new technologies, those closest to the (always rapidly changing) technology are often in the best position to envision a possible application. Therefore the research and development engineers in these companies are usually the source of possible new products, contrasting with non-technology companies where the pool of new product ideas usually comes from customers.

In any case, it is the function of marketing to match the desires of customers with the capabilities of the company, and to match the pool of new engineering-inspired product ideas in a technology company with the desires of customers. Marketing in technology companies may therefore be less concerned with creating new product ideas than with the rest of the marketing formula.

The sales of technology companies usually follow the adoption curve; the experimental, technologically sophisticated customers buy first, and other customers follow as the technology becomes more accepted and less new. Therefore a technology product's initial success depends on finding and selling to these few, unique early adaptors. Regis McKenna (*The Regis Touch*, Addison Wesley) suggests that the marketing effort to reach these early adaptors differs from marketing activities for more traditional products. His good advice includes such insights as:

- Market share is not applicable to products with no direct competition;

- The focus should be on market creation rather than market share.

- Massive promotional activities such as large advertising campaigns are not appropriate. The target audience of early adaptors is usually quite small and can be reached more effectively with a smaller scale, more focused effort.

- There is a network of opinion leaders who are the best possible promotional vehicle for the new technology product. These include consultants, editors, industry gurus, early customers, etc., and the focus of the promotional effort should be identifying and converting these opinion leaders.

I agree that market share does not initially have the same significance for new technology products as it does for more traditional products; but I maintain that the interested market often includes both the old and new way of doing what your product does. Airplanes at first did not compete with other airplanes, but with automobiles and trains. Computers at first did not compete with other computers but with manual and mechanical computation and record-keeping devices. I suggest that you should measure the market defined in a way that includes alternate ways of accomplishing the same task, and also by the amount of the new market you have created with your product.

Putting the Formula to Work in the Start-up Company

Start-up companies are generally launched after a considerable amount of time has been spent pulling together and selling a business plan. Any decent business plan has an extensive marketing section which addresses the opportunity, the competition, product positioning, customers, and promotional plans. Much of the *Understand, Predict*, and *Identify Opportunities* work has been done at this point. (If it has not, the principals had better rethink the wisdom of launching a company without that information.)

Start-up companies are also typically on a firm schedule and tight budget, and are almost entirely focused on getting the first product out the door. Once that happens they will then have the luxury to face the problems of being a small company.

This means that the focus of marketing activity in the start-up phase is mainly on marketing operations, particularly in continuing to track closely the competition and opportunity, and the *Develop* and (later) *Promote* activities. Since a great deal of the marketing planning activities were done in preparing the business plan, the company's main job now is to execute the plan. If the first product succeeds, marketing planning can begin on the subsequent products.

Putting the Formula to Work in the Consumer Goods Company

The main distinction of successful consumer goods is that they are influenced more by tastes and social trends than are industrial goods. In consumer goods companies these influences, in addition to the usual economic influences, will have to be looked at closely, particularly in the *Understand* and *Predict* areas.

For example, *Understand the Customer*, vendor criteria may have to consider—in addition to such economic factors as price—vendor reputation, purchasing convenience, and social factors such as attitudes of the public toward the vendor. To illustrate: companies that do business in certain countries or engage in certain labor practices have lost customers recently, while companies that, for example, do not test their products on animals have gained customers.

The influence of social attitudes and changing tastes applies to established product categories, such as laundry detergent and carbonated beverages, and to the creation of new product categories such as premium ice cream. For example, the creation and promotion of phosphate-free products in the established laundry detergent market is due to a social influence, while changing taste preferences have created a huge new market for premium ice cream.

Putting the Formula to Work
in the Industrial Goods Company

While there are definite exceptions, industrial goods tend to be purchased on the basis of technical performance and specifications. This situation requires special attention to the *Understand the Product* items such as how and why the product is used, and the *Promote Sales to Prospects* activities of seminars and presentations. The marketer in the industrial goods company will generally need to have a good understanding of the product's technical characteristics.

It is therefore necessary to insure that marketing positions are filled by persons possessing the appropriate level of technical expertise. In a low-tech industrial goods market, such as cardboard boxes, the appropriate technical understanding of the product can be gained by many people. By contrast, high-tech industrial goods, such as mainframe computers, may well require the expertise of a degreed engineer for effective marketing.

Putting the Formula to Work
in the Transaction Based Company

The buy/sell relationship between two businesses tends to be either transaction based or relationship based. (For an in-depth discussion of this topic, see *Winning and Keeping Industrial Customers*, Barbara Bund Jackson, Lexington Books, 1985.)

Transaction-based buyers are characterized by:

- Each product purchase is evaluated independently of others
- Short time horizons
- Small investment per purchase
- Low vendor loyalty
- Low vendor switching costs
- The purchase of simple products

The transaction buyer is motivated primarily by product features: price, terms, and delivery time. Consequently, these areas should be thoroughly researched in the *Understand the Customer* effort and given particular attention during the *Develop Products* activities. Transaction buyers can often be effectively reached through advertising, direct mail, catalogs, and other immediate inducement vehicles, and these deserve extra consideration in the *Promote the Products* activities.

Putting the Formula to Work in the Relationship-Based Company

Relationship buyers are characterized by:

- Careful evaluation of each purchase
- Long time horizons
- Large investments per purchase
- High vendor loyalty
- High vendor switching costs
- The establishment of a business partnership with a vendor.

Relationship buyers are motivated mostly by vendor stability, long term product direction, and vendor support. Consequently, the *Understand the Customer* activities need to pay particular attention to these areas. *The Develop Products* activities should focus on support requirements and service requirements, and the *Promote* activities should pay particular attention to company advertising and *Promoting Customer Partnerships*.

Putting the Formula to Work in the Early Product Life Cycle Stages

In the early stages of a product's life cycle it is generally the innovators and early adaptors who buy the product. These customers tend to be very involved with the products; they often know about a new product as soon as it is announced and may already have a detailed understanding of how it works. As a consequence of their deep involvement with the products, they will usually seek out the company with a new product in the categories that interest them.

Therefore, a strong focus for companies in the early stages of its product's life cycle should be product announcement. This is accomplished as much by *Promoting the Company* through press releases and articles, as by *Promoting the Product* through advertising. If you have done a good job in the *Understand, Develop* and planning areas you will soon have steady sales to the innovators and early adaptors, and you will be building momentum to allow your product to move along the adoption curve.

Putting the Formula to Work in the Later Product Life Cycle Stages

As the product becomes less novel and more accepted, the majority of potential customers become available. Consequently the promotional approaches that reach large audiences, such as media advertising, direct mail, and sponsorships, can play a significant role in the marketing efforts.

As a product goes through the middle stages of it's product life cycle there are usually considerably more competitors than when the product first appeared. Therefore more attention needs to be paid to *Understand the Market*, and *Understand the Competition*—promotional efforts will need to respond to competitive promotional campaigns and target the competitor's weakness. Opportunities are now more likely to be in the market development, market penetration, and concentric diversification areas.

In addition, the customers for a mature product tend to place more emphasis on attributes other than product features such as service and channel convenience.

Marketing with Science

Whenever I get a little hairbrained or disorganized on a project, a friend of mine usually calls my attention to the fact by saying, "Let's do this with a little science."

That's what this book has been about: doing marketing with science. The activity focused, information flow dependent model of marketing laid out here should give you a comprehensive checklist of marketing activities to perform and a blueprint for coordinating them.

I believe that economic progress is the great liberator, and I hope that this book on marketing may somehow contribute to it. To paraphrase Peter

Drucker: "Marketing is essentially viewing the enterprise from the viewpoint of the customer, and there is very little difference between it and the management of the enterprise as a whole."

Listing each and every individual marketing activity has been an ambitious task, and I'm sure to have missed some. I welcome your comments on this book and the model and formula presented here - please write to me in care of Avant Books.

Order Form

Thank you for purchasing *The Formula for Successful Marketing.* To order additional copies of this book or the one described below, please complete the form at the bottom of this page or telephone 1-800-SLAWSON.

Another Avant Leadership Guide:

Talking Your Way to the Top

The Executive's Guide to Public Speaking by John W. Osborne

You will learn how to:

- Rid yourself of fear and anxiety.
- Improve your self-confidence.
- Make your words sparkle.
- Keep your audience interested.
- Be the hit of business and social events.

Name _____

Address _____

City _____ State _____ Zip _____

Qty.	Title	Price ea.	Total	
	Talking Your Way to the Top	$8.95		
	The Formula for Successful Marketing	$8.95		

U.S. SHIPPING Books are shipped UPS except when a post office box is given as a delivery address.	Subtotal	
	Sales Tax: CA residents add 7.25%	
	Shipping & Handling: $3.00 for first book, 50 cents for each additional book.	
	TOTAL	

FORM OF PAYMENT

☐ Visa ☐ MasterCard ☐ Check

Card #: ⬚⬚⬚⬚ ⬚⬚⬚⬚ ⬚⬚⬚⬚ ⬚⬚⬚⬚

Expiration date: _____

Signature: _____

Mail this order form to:

Avant Books®
Slawson Communications, Inc.
165 Vallecitos de Oro
San Marcos, CA 92069-1436

619/744-2299